Married but Happily Single

ARROON GAWALLI

BLUEROSE PUBLISHERS
India | U.K.

Copyright © Arroon Gawalli 2024

All rights reserved by author. No part of this publication may be reproduced, stored in a retrieval system or transmitted in any form or by any means, electronic, mechanical, photocopying, recording or otherwise, without the prior permission of the author. Although every precaution has been taken to verify the accuracy of the information contained herein, the publisher assumes no responsibility for any errors or omissions. No liability is assumed for damages that may result from the use of information contained within.

BlueRose Publishers takes no responsibility for any damages, losses, or liabilities that may arise from the use or misuse of the information, products, or services provided in this publication.

For permissions requests or inquiries regarding this publication, please contact:

BLUEROSE PUBLISHERS
www.BlueRoseONE.com
info@bluerosepublishers.com
+91 8882 898 898
+4407342408967

ISBN: 978-93-5704-791-3

Cover design: Muskan Sachdeva
Typesetting: Rohit

First Edition: January 2024

Preface

Married but Happily Single: Navigating the Complexities of Modern Indian Marriages

In the vibrant heart of Mumbai, a city that embodies both the essence of tradition and the pulse of modernity, the narrative of 'Married but Happily Single' takes on a new significance. This book delves deep into the tumultuous journey of Meera and Raj, a couple whose story unveils the profound generational chasm that plagues many millennials today.

The title of this book, seemingly paradoxical, encapsulates a struggle that resonates deeply with the millennial generation. It's a journey through the labyrinth of modern Indian marriages, where the collision of two distinct generations, each with its unique set of challenges, often results in the unraveling of marital bonds.

In today's rapidly changing society, one generation finds itself rooted in traditional values and customs, while another is navigating the complexities of an internet-savvy life and the demands of a fiercely competitive market. Bridging the gap between these worlds becomes a formidable task. Millennials are caught in the crossfire, struggling to find common ground, and as a consequence, divorces have become an unfortunate outcome.

Meera and Raj's story is not just a love story; it's a reflection of the generational schism that plagues modern Indian marriages. Their journey embodies the relentless quest for individuality within the confines of societal expectations, the pain of separation, and the exhilaration of rediscovery. Their story illustrates the stark reality that modern Indian marriages are vulnerable to the generational divide.

'Married but Happily Single' stands as a beacon of hope amidst these turbulent waters. It serves as a guide for millennials grappling with the complexities of marriage, offering insights into navigating the challenges posed by the generation gap. This book is a roadmap towards achieving a deeper and more fulfilling marital union by striking a harmonious balance between individuality and togetherness. As you embark on this journey through the pages of this book, you'll bear witness to the highs and lows of Meera and Raj's matrimonial life. More importantly, you'll gain a profound understanding of the generational struggles they face, which are symptomatic of the larger issue plaguing millennial marriages. 'Married but Happily Single' offers a solution, a message of hope that through understanding, communication, and compromise, it is indeed possible to be married yet remain happily single in spirit, thus bridging the gap and forging stronger, more resilient bonds.

About the Author

Arroon Gawalli: A Voice for Emotional Independence in Marriage

Arroon Gawalli emerges as a poignant voice in the landscape of modern relationship literature with his, 'Married but Happily Single.' Residing in the bustling city of Mumbai, Arroon brings to the table a rich tapestry of experiences and observations from the myriad marital stories unfolding in this dynamic metropolis.

Arroon's deep interest in the psychology of relationships and his keen eye for the nuances of human emotions have fueled his passion for exploring the complex dynamics of marriage in the Indian context. He combines his psychological insights with a compelling narrative style to weave a story that is both engaging and enlightening.

'Married but Happily Single' is born out of Arroon's desire to address the often unspoken emotional struggles in marriages. He empathetically navigates through the journey of Meera and Raj, offering readers a lens to view their marital challenges and triumphs. Arroon's narrative is a heartfelt dialogue with his readers, addressing the need for emotional independence and personal growth within the sanctity of marriage.

In his book, Arroon aims to empower individuals to find a balance between their personal aspirations and their commitments as partners. He advocates for the idea that maintaining one's individuality in marriage is not only possible but essential for a fulfilling and enduring union. Through 'Married but Happily Single,' Arroon aspires to inspire a new paradigm in marital relationships, one where emotional independence is seen as the cornerstone of a happy, healthy, and harmonious partnership.

Contents

Serendipitous Encounter 1
Melodies of Mumbai.. 7
Symphony of Hearts 13
Through Seasons of Love...17
A Simple Promise 21
Unfolding Together..27
Amidst Tensions and Ties 33
The Outside Pressures...39
Unravelling Expectations...45
The Unspoken Betrayal..49
The Tumultuous Journey to Separation 53
The Heartrending Farewell 57
Closure: Echoes of a Lost Forever 61
Echoes of the Past..65
A Chance Reunion in Shadows of Past....................73
New Horizons...79
The Whispers of Heart and Soul 83
The Art of Letting Go..87
Paths of Rediscovery..91
Serendipitous Reencounter at the Book Café 95
Rekindled Bonds and New Beginnings....................99
Reunion Amidst Reservations..................................103
The Second Wedding - A Bold Statement..............107
Building an Empire – A Culinary and Design Odyssey......113

Harmony in Togetherness and Individuality 117
Redefining Relationships in Contemporary India 121

Married but Happily Single:
A New Paradigm... *124*

Concluding Thoughts:
A Message of Hope and Resilience..................................... *126*

Understanding the Essence of Marriage:
The Journey of Meera and Raj... *127*

Closing Remarks by Author Arroon Gawalli:
Embracing the Paradox of 'Married but Happily Single'
- A Beacon of Hope.. *130*

Serendipitous Encounter

Mumbai's monsoon had draped the city in a cloak of verdant freshness, the rains bringing life to every nook and cranny. It was in this season of new beginnings that Raj first caught a glimpse of Meera. The setting was a quaint book café in Bandra, where the aroma of rain on concrete mingled with the scent of brewing coffee and aged paper.

Meera was absorbed in a book, her face illuminated by the soft, diffused light filtering through the café's front window. She seemed an embodiment of serenity amid the city's usual cacophony. The gentle tapping of the rain against the window provided a rhythmic backdrop to her silent reading.

Raj, on the other hand, was there for an entirely different reason. His friend owned the café and had called him over to discuss the possibility of hosting educational workshops for children. But as Raj stepped in, shaking off the droplets clinging to his jacket, his attention was unwittingly stolen by Meera's presence.

Their eyes met, and for a moment, the world seemed to stand still. The café's hustle and bustle faded into the background. Meera's gaze was questioning, a hint of curiosity flickering within. Raj offered a tentative smile, an unspoken greeting between two strangers.

Compelled by a force he couldn't name; Raj approached her table. "Is the book as captivating as it seems?" he asked, gesturing to the novel in her hands.

Meera looked up, her initial surprise softening into a smile. "It's an old favourite. It's always different each time I read it."

The conversation flowed effortlessly from there. They spoke of literature, the nuances of character development, and the art of storytelling. As they conversed, they found themselves delving into personal ambitions and life philosophies. Raj was fascinated by Meera's perspective—a blend of poetic idealism and stark realism.

The hours slipped by uncounted as the rain outside lessened to a drizzle. When they finally parted, they did so with the promise to continue their discussion. As Raj walked back into the city's heartbeat, the café behind him, he couldn't help but feel that the day had offered him more than he had anticipated.

That night, Raj found himself thinking about Meera, about the unexpected connection they seemed to share. There was something about her that challenged and complemented him simultaneously. He made up his mind to see her again.

The following day, as the city of Mumbai bustled with its usual fervour, the skies cleared to a canvas of blue. Raj couldn't shake off the image of Meera's animated expressions as she talked about her favourite author. He found himself back at the café, under the pretext of finalizing the workshop plans, but a part of him hoped for another encounter.

As if the universe was conspiring, Meera walked through the door once again, her presence a pleasant surprise that brightened the café's atmosphere. She caught sight of Raj and smiled, her approach this time deliberate.

"It seems the rain has decided to give us a break," she remarked, settling down at the table next to his with a fresh cup of coffee in hand.

Raj grinned, "Or maybe it's giving us a chance to continue our conversation from yesterday."

Their dialogue resumed, this time meandering through topics beyond books — the essence of Mumbai, their favourite monsoon memories, and the dreams that the city inspired in them. It was as if they were old friends, comfortable and familiar in each other's company.

As the café's clock ticked towards noon, Raj realized he didn't want this unexpected meeting to be their last. "Would you like to meet again, perhaps for a walk at the Colaba ? It's quite happning during the evenings," he suggested, hopeful.

Meera nodded, her eyes bright with interest. "I'd like that. It's a date then."

They exchanged numbers, a formal acknowledgment of the bond that was beginning to form. That evening, as Raj waited for her text, he felt a twinge of excitement, a prelude to possibilities that could unfold from this burgeoning connection.

Meera didn't keep him waiting long. Her message popped up on his screen just as the night began to envelop the city, bringing with it the cool breeze from the sea.

"Tomorrow at 5? Colaba awaits," her message read.

Raj's fingers danced over the keypad, "Tomorrow at 5 it is."

Their texts over the next day were sporadic but filled with anticipation. They shared snippets of their day, a photo of the sunrise from Meera's terrace, a quote from Raj's current read, small tokens of a growing intimacy.

Melodies of Mumbai

As Raj left the cozy café, the drizzle outside seemed to match his thoughtful mood. The encounter with Meera had stirred something within him, a sense of excitement mingled with a newfound curiosity. He couldn't shake off the image of her expressive eyes, so full of life and intellect.

As the last message from Meera faded from his phone screen, Raj found himself enveloped in a sense of anticipation. Their conversation, which had begun in the quaint solitude of the café, was now set to continue against the vibrant backdrop of Mumbai. He couldn't help but feel that their next meeting might unfold new layers of their burgeoning connection.

The next day, the vibrant streets of Colaba Causeway, with their lively blend of colours, sounds, and scents, set the perfect stage for Raj and Meera's burgeoning connection. Raj waited with a mix of eagerness and nerves near the old Regal Cinema, the city's pulse echoing his own heightened heartbeat.

As Meera approached, her presence seemed to calm the chaos around them. She greeted him with a warm smile, her eyes shining with a mixture of excitement and comfort. "Every time I come here, it feels like stepping into a different world," she remarked, taking in the surroundings.

Raj, buoyed by her enthusiasm, replied, "And yet, there's a familiarity in its chaos, kind of like the unpredictability of our meeting."

Their stroll along the Causeway was punctuated with laughter and playful banter. At a colourful scarf stall, Raj teased Meera, "If you were to choose a colour that represents you, what would it be?"

Meera, holding a deep blue scarf against the light, said thoughtfully, "Blue, perhaps. Deep and contemplative, but also calm and reassuring." She looked at Raj, a playful challenge in her eyes. "Your turn, what colour are you?"

"Green, I think," Raj responded with a smile. "It speaks of growth, new beginnings. Like what we're experiencing right now."

As they continued their walk, the conversation flowed effortlessly. They talked about everything from their favourite Mumbai street foods to the monsoon memories that defined their childhoods. Raj was captivated by Meera's insights and perspectives, finding himself drawn to her unique blend of strength and vulnerability.

As the sky began to paint itself in hues of orange and pink, they made their way to Marine Drive. Sitting on the sea-facing promenade, they shared personal stories against the backdrop of the gently crashing waves. Raj spoke candidly about his family's legacy and the weight of expectations that came with it, while Meera opened up about her aspirations to leave a lasting impact on Mumbai's architecture.

The conversation deepened as the night wore on. They discussed their dreams, fears, and the thrill of new beginnings. Raj was struck by Meera's determination and her passion for her craft. "It's rare to meet someone who not only dreams but also has the courage to chase those dreams," he said, admiration evident in his voice.

Meera responded with a soft laugh, "And it's equally rare to find someone who understands and appreciates that pursuit. I feel like you get me, Raj, more than most people do."

Their exchange was filled with moments of eye contact that spoke volumes, the unspoken connection between them growing stronger with each word. They shared not just conversations, but also silent understandings, comfortable in each other's presence.

As they reluctantly said their goodbyes, the promise of future meetings lingered in the air. "I'm really glad we met, Raj. There's something about you that feels... right," Meera confessed, her voice low.

Raj, feeling a similar sentiment, replied, "I couldn't agree more, Meera. Here's to exploring where 'us' leads." Their smiles, full of unspoken promises, lit up the night.

As the night deepened around them, casting Marine Drive in a soft, ambient glow, Raj and Meera knew it was time to part ways. Their conversation had meandered through the landscapes of their lives, each revelation bringing them closer. Now, standing by the sea, the sound of waves echoing their steady heartbeats, neither wanted the evening to end.

"When can we do this again?" Raj asked, his voice tinged with hope. The thought of waiting to see Meera again filled him with a mix of anticipation and impatience.

Meera's response came with a warm, reassuring smile that lit up her eyes in the twilight. "Soon," she said, her tone reflecting a promise. "We shouldn't make Mumbai wait too long for the next chapter of our story."

Their farewell was a lingering one, filled with unspoken emotions and a mutual reluctance to let go of the moment. As they finally parted, there was a sense of something significant just beginning, a story that was theirs to write in the heart of a city that had seen countless tales unfold.

Symphony of Hearts

The sun was just beginning to dip below the horizon, casting a golden glow over Mumbai as Raj waited outside the Jehangir Art Gallery for Meera. They had decided to explore the city's artistic side for their next meeting. Each date seemed to add a new dimension to their rapidly blossoming relationship.

Meera arrived, her eyes brightening as she spotted Raj. "I've always loved this place," she said, her voice tinged with excitement. "Art has a way of speaking without words."

As they wandered through the gallery, admiring the diverse array of artworks, their conversation flowed effortlessly. Raj paused in front of a vibrant abstract painting. "What does this one says to you?" he asked, curious to hear her interpretation.

Meera studied the painting for a moment. "It speaks of chaos and harmony coexisting. Much like our city, don't you think?" she replied, her gaze shifting from the painting to Raj.

He nodded, impressed by her insight. "I couldn't agree more. There's something about the way it all just fits together, even in the midst of chaos."

Their shared appreciation for the arts led them to a cozy café nearby, where they continued their discussion over coffee. The conversation soon turned personal, delving into their aspirations and the challenges they faced in pursuing them.

In the cozy ambience of the café, Raj and Meera delved into conversations about their professional aspirations, each sharing their passions and dreams. Raj, with a deep-rooted love for culinary arts, spoke of his dream to open a fusion restaurant. "I envision a place where every dish narrates a story, blending traditional and contemporary flavors," he shared, his eyes reflecting his culinary aspirations.

Meera, listening intently, shared her own professional goals. "As an architect, I aim to design buildings that are more than structures; they should reflect the soul of the city, telling stories through their designs," she explained, her voice filled with passion for her craft.

This exchange in the café highlighted their shared drive for creativity and success in their careers. Raj, the aspiring chef with innovative ideas for a unique dining experience, and Meera, the architect with a vision to impact Mumbai's skyline, both saw their work as an extension of their artistic expression. Their mutual respect for each other's ambitions added a meaningful layer to their relationship, making them not just partners in love but also in their journey towards professional fulfilment.

The café began to empty as they lost track of time, engrossed in each other's company. Realizing how late it had gotten, Raj suggested a walk along the Marine Drive promenade.

As they strolled by the sea, the city lights reflecting off the water, Meera took a deep breath. "You know, every time I'm with you, it feels like I'm discovering a new part of Mumbai... and a new part of myself."

Raj reached for her hand, holding it gently. "Meera, I feel the same. There's something about us that just feels right, like we're meant to be on this journey together."

Their conversation was filled with laughter, shared dreams, and the occasional comfortable silence. The evening culminated in a promise to meet again soon, with both sensing that what was unfolding between them was something profoundly special.

As they finally said goodbye, Raj felt a surge of emotion. "Meera, I... I really enjoy spending time with you. It's something I've come to look forward to more than anything."

Meera's smile was soft, yet it held a depth of emotion. "Raj, I feel the same. There's an ease and a joy in being with you that I haven't found before."

Through Seasons of Love

As Raj and Meera journeyed through their six months of dating, each date seamlessly wove into the next, creating a beautiful tapestry of shared experiences that deepened their bond.

Their adventure began with a day trip to the Sanjay Gandhi National Park, where the natural beauty of the trails served as a backdrop for their growing closeness. Walking through the verdant paths, they shared stories and laughter, each step bringing them closer. This trip laid the foundation for their appreciation of simple joys and the beauty of nature – themes that would recur in their relationship.

The tranquillity of the park was soon contrasted by the vibrant energy of the Kala Ghoda Arts Festival. As they immersed themselves in the cultural festivities, their connection deepened, each appreciating the other's insights and perspectives on art and life. The festival was a canvas that reflected their growing understanding and appreciation of each other's interests and passions.

These larger outings were interspersed with quieter moments, such as evenings spent at Meera's apartment. Here, in the comfort of home, they cooked together, an activity that became a cherished ritual. Each meal they prepared was more than just food; it was a symbol of their harmony and teamwork. These evenings of cooking and watching films were intimate interludes that balanced their more adventurous dates, strengthening their bond in everyday settings.

The spontaneity of their relationship was marked by impromptu outings – a sudden craving for street food, a drive along the Sea Link, or a visit to a new café. These unplanned adventures added an element of surprise and excitement, showing them how well they adapted to each other's whims and fancies. Each spontaneous plan was a thread that connected back to their earlier dates, a continuation of the joy and exploration they found in each other's company.

As they celebrated their six-month anniversary, they chose a serene beach setting, a nod to their first outing to the national park and the many walks they had since enjoyed. Sitting together, watching the sunset, they reflected on the journey they had shared. The ease with which one date transitioned into the next, the way their experiences interconnected, revealed the depth of their compatibility and understanding.

As the sun dipped below the horizon, casting a warm, golden hue over the beach, Raj and Meera sat in comfortable silence, hand in hand, reflecting on the beautiful journey they had shared.

Breaking the silence, Raj turned to Meera, his eyes soft with affection. "You know, these six months have felt like a lifetime of happiness," he said gently.

Meera smiled, leaning her head on his shoulder. "And yet, it's just the beginning, Raj. I can't wait to see what the future holds for us," she replied, her voice filled with love and anticipation.

They sat there for a few more moments, watching as the last of the sun's rays disappeared, leaving a sky painted in shades of pink and purple. In this peaceful ending to the day, they found a promise of new beginnings, a future filled with love and shared adventures.

A Simple Promise

Following the heartfelt experiences and shared moments, Raj felt a profound certainty in his heart. It was a clear, starry evening in Mumbai, and he had planned something simple yet meaningful to express his deepest feelings to Meera. The location was Bandstand Promenade, a place that had witnessed many of their leisurely walks and deep conversations.

Meera, intrigued by Raj's message saying he had a surprise for her, met him at their favorite spot by the sea. The night air was filled with the soothing sound of waves, and the distant city lights flickered like stars brought down to earth.

"There's something special about this place," Meera said as she approached Raj, who was waiting with a nervous smile.

"It's where I realized how much you mean to me," Raj replied, his voice laced with emotion. He took her hand, leading her to a bench overlooking the sea.

They sat together, watching the gentle ebb and flow of the waves. Raj took a deep breath, gathering his thoughts. "Meera, these past months with you have been the happiest of my life. I've discovered joy in the smallest moments because they were shared with you."

Meera looked at him, her eyes reflecting the sincerity in his words.

"I may not have grand gestures or eloquent speeches, but what I have is a heart that truly, deeply cares for you," Raj continued, his gaze never leaving hers. "I love you, Meera. I love your laughter, your passion, your kindness. Every moment with you feels like a piece of a beautiful dream."

Meera's eyes glistened with unshed tears, her hand tightening around his.

"Tonight, under this sky, beside this sea, I want to ask you something simple, yet it holds all my hopes and dreams," Raj said, his voice steady yet full of emotion. He reached into his pocket, pulling out a small, elegantly simple ring.

"Meera, will you be with me in this journey of life? Will you marry me?" he asked, his heart in his eyes.

The world around them seemed to pause, the waves whispering in anticipation. Meera's response was a soft whisper, yet it carried the weight of all the love she felt. "Yes, Raj. I will."

As they embraced, the simplicity of the moment made it all the more profound. There were no grand declarations, no audience to witness, just two hearts promising each other a lifetime of love and companionship...

As the night deepened, Raj and Meera remained seated on the bench, hand in hand, lost in a comfortable silence. The sea in front of them, vast and seemingly infinite, was a testament to the depth of what they had just shared. The stars above shone brightly, blessing the new chapter they were about to embark upon together.

Eventually, Meera broke the silence. "I always believed that the best moments in life are the simplest ones," she said softly, her head resting on Raj's shoulder. "Tonight proves that."

Raj squeezed her hand gently. "I wanted this to be a memory we'd always cherish, a moment of just us and our love, no distractions."

They stayed there for a while longer, savoring the tranquillity of the moment. The night around them was a cocoon, holding their newly promised future within its serene embrace.

As they finally stood to leave, Raj wrapped his arm around Meera, and they slowly walked back, their steps in sync. The promenade was quieter now, the bustle of the city a distant hum. They talked about immediate plans, about telling their families and friends, but more importantly, about the many dreams they now hoped to fulfil together.

The next day dawned bright and clear, a fitting metaphor for the new beginning in Raj and Meera's life. Raj woke up to a flurry of messages from Meera, each one expressing her excitement and love. The reality of their engagement brought a sense of joy and responsibility he had never felt before.

They decided to meet for a celebratory breakfast at their favorite café – the very place where it all began. The café held a special place in their hearts, a reminder of their journey from strangers to soulmates.

As they sat across from each other, sharing a meal and laughter, there was a palpable sense of happiness surrounding them. They discussed plans, both immediate and long-term, weaving their aspirations and hopes into the fabric of their future together.

Meera, looking across the table at Raj, felt a surge of affection. "Do you realize this is where our story started? And now, here we are, planning our life together."

Raj reached across the table, taking her hand. "It feels like destiny, doesn't it? Like all roads were meant to lead us here."

The discussion closes with Raj and Meera making plans, not just for their wedding but for the life they intended to build together. Their conversation was a blend of excitement, love, and a touch of the inevitable nervousness that comes with stepping into a shared future. In the heart of Mumbai, surrounded by the familiar sights and sounds of the café, they toasted to their love – a love that had grown quietly but resolutely, ready now to bloom in full.

Unfolding Together

Over the course of six months, Raj and Meera's relationship evolved gracefully, each day weaving a deeper connection between them. Their journey was not marked by grand gestures or dramatic moments, but rather the quiet, steady growth of love and understanding.

The essence of their relationship lay in the simple things – evening walks along Juhu Beach, where the setting sun painted the sky in hues of orange and pink, quiet dinners at their favorite restaurants, and long conversations that stretched into the night. These moments, seemingly ordinary, became the foundation of their deepening bond.

They found joy in exploring Mumbai together, discovering hidden gems in the city that had become the backdrop of their love story. Whether it was trying out new cafes, visiting local markets, or just driving around the city, each experience brought them closer, turning the mundane into something special.

As they grew more comfortable with each other, their conversations delved deeper, exploring not just their hopes and dreams but also their fears and vulnerabilities. These talks often took place in the quiet of Raj's living room or Meera's balcony, where they shared their innermost thoughts under the canopy of Mumbai's night sky.

Their relationship was not without its challenges, but they faced them together, with patience and understanding. The disagreements they had were resolved with heartfelt discussions, each learning and growing from these experiences. It was through these challenges that they realized the strength of their bond, a bond that was resilient and enduring.

The six-month mark of their relationship was quietly celebrated with a candlelit dinner at home. They cooked together, laughing and talking as they prepared their meal. It was a simple evening, yet it held a profound significance for both of them. As they sat down to eat, they reflected on their journey so far.

"Six months feels both long and short, doesn't it?" Meera mused as she sipped her wine.

"It does," Raj agreed, his eyes on her. "But every moment has been worth it. You've made my life so much richer, Meera."

Their conversation that night was a reaffirmation of their feelings, a mutual recognition of the love that had grown between them. It was a love built on shared experiences, mutual respect, and a deep understanding of each other.

As the evening gave way to the gentle embrace of the night, Raj and Meera stood together on the balcony, their hands clasped, looking out at the sprawling city of Mumbai. The city lights twinkled like distant stars, mirroring the quiet glow in their hearts. In the soft breeze and the tranquility of the moment, there was a sense of profound understanding and deep connection between them.

Meera leaned her head against Raj's shoulder, her voice a soft whisper against the backdrop of the city's distant hum. "Raj, do you ever think about our future? Where this journey is taking us?"

Raj, his gaze still fixed on the horizon, tightened his hold on her hand gently. "I think about it all the time," he confessed. "About us, about a future where we're together, facing whatever life throws at us. With you, Meera, even the uncertainties seem bearable."

There was a weight to his words, a sincerity that resonated with the truth of his feelings. Meera looked up, her eyes meeting his. "I feel the same, Raj. These past months with you have been the most real, the most beautiful part of my life. It feels like we're building something that's meant to last."

In the soft glow of the balcony lights, Raj's face held a look of determination and love. "Meera, I've never been surer of anything as I am of us. Maybe it's time we think about taking the next step. About making our commitment to each other more... permanent."

The word 'permanent' lingered in the air, a testament to the depth of their bond. Meera's heart raced at the implication, a mix of joy and anticipation filling her. "Are you talking about marriage, Raj?" she asked, a hopeful note in her voice.

"Yes," Raj replied, his voice steady. "Marriage. I can't imagine my life without you, Meera. I want us to start thinking about a future where we're not just partners but husband and wife."

Meera's response was a radiant smile, a smile that spoke of her love and her readiness to embark on this new journey with him. "I want that too, Raj. More than anything."

Raj and Meera holding each other, their hearts in sync with the rhythm of the city around them. In the comfort of their embrace, they knew they were ready to take the leap into a shared future. Mumbai, the city that had seen their love blossom, now stood witness to their decision to unite their lives. It was a love that had been tested and had triumphed, a love ready to transition into the sacred bond of marriage.

Amidst Tensions and Ties

In the heart of Mumbai, under a canopy of stars, Meera and Raj found themselves navigating the rough waters of wedding preparations, each day bringing a new challenge, testing their resolve and the strength of their bond.

"Why won't they just be happy for us?" Meera lamented one evening, her voice laced with frustration and sadness. They sat in Raj's apartment, surrounded by a sea of wedding catalogues and plans. Her family's indifference weighed heavily on her heart, their self-centred attitudes casting a long shadow over what should have been the happiest time of her life.

Raj reached across the table, taking her hand in his. "We knew this wouldn't be easy," he said, trying to offer comfort. "But remember, we're in this together. Your family's indifference won't change what we have."

Despite Raj's words, the tension was palpable. Meera's struggles with her stepmother and sisters over the financial aspects of the wedding were draining, each conversation a battle of wills. And for Raj, the disapproval from his own family, who couldn't look past Meera's background and current family situation, added another layer of stress.

One evening, as they sat overlooking the city from Raj's balcony, Meera's phone buzzed with yet another demanding message from her stepmother. She read it and sighed, a mixture of anger and helplessness in her eyes. "It's like they only see me as a ticket to their own gains," she whispered.

Raj, feeling a surge of protectiveness, squeezed her hand. "Let me help. I can't stand seeing you this way." His offer to assist financially was both a gesture of solidarity and a testament to his commitment.

But this decision wasn't without its repercussions. Raj's own family viewed his support as imprudent, widening the rift that had been forming. "You're being taken advantage of," his aunt warned him one day. "You need to think of your future, not just of Meera's problems."

These words stung Raj, but his resolve didn't waver. "My future is with Meera," he responded firmly, though the conflict with his family left him torn.

The days leading up to the wedding were a blur of arrangements and emotional upheaval. The lack of enthusiasm from Meera's family was starkly contrasted by the quiet, albeit reluctant, support from Raj's side. The couple often found themselves consoling each other, their love the only constant in a sea of uncertainty.

Finally, the wedding day arrived. It was a bittersweet celebration, the joy of their union mingled with the sorrow of familial discord. As they stood together, exchanging vows, their voices steady but their hearts heavy, they knew this was a testament to their love – a love that had weathered the storm of societal and familial pressures.

As the final notes of the wedding music faded into the night, Meera and Raj stood side by side, their hands clasped tightly. The glow from the strings of lights that adorned the venue cast a soft, ethereal light on their faces, reflecting the myriad of emotions that played across them. They had just embarked on a lifelong journey together, a journey that had begun with a simple, serendipitous encounter and had now culminated in their union as husband and wife.

The air was filled with a sense of accomplishment and a tinge of wistfulness. They had managed to overcome the obstacles that life, with its unpredictable nature, had thrown their way. The indifference of Meera's family and the underlying tensions with Raj's had tested them, forging their bond in the fire of adversity.

As they looked into each other's eyes, there was an unspoken promise that resonated between them - a vow of enduring support, unwavering loyalty, and a love that transcended the trials they had faced. This moment was theirs, a testament to their resilience and the depth of their feelings for one another.

Meera, her eyes shimmering with unshed tears, felt a surge of emotions. The wedding, with all its imperfections and challenges, was more beautiful than she had ever imagined because it symbolized their victory over the trials they had faced together. "We did it, Raj," she whispered, her voice a mixture of joy and awe. "Despite everything, we did it."

Raj, with a gentle smile, drew her closer. "Yes, we did, Meera. And we'll keep doing it, every day, for the rest of our lives." His voice was steady, imbued with the certainty and depth of his commitment.

Around them, the remnants of the celebration whispered stories of the day - laughter, tears, dances, and toasts. But in that moment, nothing else mattered. They were in their own world, a sanctuary built on love, understanding, and mutual respect.

The night sky above them was a canvas of stars, each twinkle a witness to their union. The gentle breeze that swept across the venue seemed to carry their hopes and dreams for the future - dreams of building a life together where they could be true to themselves, yet united in their journey.

As they stepped forward, ready to begin their life as a married couple, there was a sense of completeness. The wedding might have ended, but their story was just beginning - a story of two individuals, committed to not just loving each other, but also cherishing and nurturing their individual identities.

The Outside Pressures

The golden sun dipped beneath the horizon of Krabi's pristine beaches as Meera and Raj walked hand in hand, their footsteps synchronizing with the rhythmic ebb and flow of the waves. The first three months of their marriage had been nothing short of magical, filled with shared laughter, whispered dreams, and an unspoken promise of forever. Their honeymoon in Krabi and Phuket was a continuation of this bliss, a bliss painted in the vibrant colors of love and new beginnings.

One evening, as they sat watching the sunset from their beachfront villa, Meera leaned against Raj. "Can we just stay in this moment forever?" she murmured, her eyes reflecting the hues of the setting sun.

Raj wrapped his arm around her, "I wish we could. But remember, every day with you is like a honeymoon, regardless of where we are."

Their days were spent exploring hidden coves, indulging in local cuisine, and making plans for their future. In these moments, they found a deep connection that transcended the everyday.

However, as they returned to the reality of Mumbai, the cocoon of their honeymoon began to unravel, revealing the challenges of married life. The initial euphoria gradually gave way to the mundane routines and responsibilities that they had previously overlooked.

Small disagreements, once dismissed as insignificant, started to surface. A forgotten dinner date, differing opinions on household matters, and the pressure of balancing work and personal life began to strain their perfect harmony.

"Raj, can we talk about how we're managing our schedules? I feel like we're not prioritizing our time together," Meera brought up one evening, concern lacing her voice.

Raj, preoccupied with his ambitions and familial responsibilities, responded, "I know it's tough, Meera. But you understand how important this is, right? We need to make some sacrifices."

These conversations were new territory for them, a stark contrast to their earlier, carefree exchanges. The realization that marriage was more than just love – that it was also about compromise, understanding, and sometimes, sacrifice – began to dawn on them.

External pressures further complicated their situation. Meera's family, who had been distant and unsupportive during the wedding, now seemed to have endless expectations, often hinting at financial assistance. Meera found herself torn between her independence and the traditional role her family expected her to play.

Raj faced his own set of challenges. The legacy of his father's educational institution loomed over him, a constant reminder of the expectations his family had. His attempts to balance his entrepreneurial dreams with these obligations often left him feeling stretched thin.

Moreover, Raj's family's idealistic expectations from Meera as a daughter-in-law created an additional layer of tension. Meera, with her independent spirit and modern outlook, struggled to fit into the traditional mold. This clash of values brought to light the differences in their upbringings and the adjustments required in their married life.

As they lay in bed one night, the gap between them felt wider than ever. "We're from two different worlds, aren't we?" Meera whispered into the darkness.

Raj turned to face her, "Maybe. But we chose to be in the same world, remember? We'll figure this out, together."

In the dimly lit confines of their bedroom, a tension hung in the air, palpable and heavy. Meera sat by the window, her gaze lost in the chaotic beauty of Mumbai's nightscape, but her mind was far away, ensnared in a turmoil of unmet expectations and growing restlessness.

Raj watched her, the silence between them stretching like a chasm. He finally spoke, his voice a mix of concern and confusion, "Meera, what's going on? You seem... distant."

Meera turned, her expression a complex tapestry of frustration and independence. "I thought marriage would be different, Raj. I thought I would still be me, but it feels like I'm losing myself, being forced into a mold that doesn't fit."

Raj's brow furrowed in distress. "I don't understand, Meera. I thought we were happy. What mold are you talking about?"

"It's everything, Raj!" Meera's voice rose, a tinge of desperation lacing her words. "Your family, their expectations of me, the traditional roles... I feel suffocated. I need my space, my identity. I can't just be a daughter-in-law, a wife. I need to be Meera!"

Raj moved closer, trying to bridge the gap, but Meera recoiled slightly, her need for space more than physical. "I respect your need for independence, Meera, but we're in this together. Can't we find a balance?"

Meera shook her head, her eyes reflecting a tumult of emotions. "I don't know, Raj. Right now, it feels like we're on two different paths. I need to figure out who I am in this marriage, if I even fit in."

The conversation, laced with misunderstanding and a clash of expectations, marked a turning point. Raj, struggling to comprehend the extent of Meera's internal struggle, felt a growing sense of helplessness. Meera, grappling with her sense of identity within the confines of her new role, found herself withdrawing, building walls that Raj found hard to penetrate.

As the night deepened, they lay in bed, side by side yet miles apart, each lost in a maelstrom of thoughts and emotions. The once harmonious rhythm of their relationship was now discordant, the melody of their love overshadowed by the cacophony of unmet expectations and aching desire for individuality.

Unravelling Expectations

In the evolving narrative of their marriage, Meera and Raj found themselves navigating through a labyrinth of challenges. Their union, once a harmonious blend of love and understanding, was now strained under the weight of unfulfilled expectations and clashing ideals.

The discord became evident one evening at Raj's family gathering. Meera, dressed in a traditional saree, felt out of place amidst the flurry of cultural rituals. Her discomfort caught the eye of Raj's aunt, Mrs. Desai, who remarked sharply, "Meera, these traditions are the essence of our family. It's important to embrace them."

Raj, witnessing the scene, felt torn. His silence was a tightrope walk between his loyalty to his roots and the love he had for Meera.

Later, in the privacy of their apartment, the day's events unraveled into an argument. Meera's frustration was palpable. "I can't lose myself in these traditions, Raj. I was never part of them," she said, her voice laced with a yearning for the independence she once cherished.

Raj, struggling to balance his familial duties with his wife's aspirations, responded, "Isn't marriage about compromises, Meera? Can't you try to fit in a little?"

The conversation spiraled, touching upon more than just the evening's events. It was about Meera feeling constrained in her new role as a wife, missing the freedom of her earlier life. It was about Raj, feeling the pressure to uphold his family's legacy while supporting his wife's independence.

The rift widened on their first anniversary. Raj, consumed by his career aspirations, forgot their special day, leaving Meera feeling neglected and alone. When confronted, Raj's response, strained from professional pressure, lacked the warmth and understanding that Meera needed.

"You're always so caught up in your work, Raj. Where do I fit into this life of yours?" Meera's words were a mix of hurt and longing for the connection they once shared.

Raj, too stressed to respond empathetically, retorted, "You know how important this project is. I'm doing this for us, Meera."

But for Meera, it was more than a forgotten anniversary. It symbolized a deeper neglect, a chasm that had developed between her expectations of married life and the reality she was living.

As the night deepened, Meera and Raj found themselves lost in a sea of silent contemplation, each on their side of the bed, a gulf of unspoken grievances between them. Meera's mind wandered to the days of her solitude, a time marked by freedom and self-sufficiency, now a stark contrast to her present life entwined with Raj and his family's expectations.

Raj, his eyes fixed on the shadowy ceiling, pondered over the complexities that marriage had unfolded. The love that had once seemed enough to overcome any obstacle now appeared fragile under the relentless weight of familial pressures and contrasting lifestyles.

In the quiet of the night, the words of their families resonated with a haunting clarity. "We told you so," echoed in their minds, a chorus of disapproval that they had once defied in the name of love. It was a painful acknowledgment that perhaps their families' concerns about their differing backgrounds and values weren't baseless after all.

The Unspoken Betrayal

The already fragile fabric of Meera and Raj's relationship faced a severe test when Raj unearthed a secret that Meera had been concealing, a revelation that threatened to shake the very foundations of their marriage.

The secret came to light one evening in a rather mundane manner. Raj, rummaging through a shared drawer for some documents, stumbled upon a sealed envelope tucked away at the back. It was addressed to Meera, but the sender's name was unfamiliar to him. Driven by a mix of curiosity and a nagging unease, he opened it.

Inside, he found a series of photographs and a letter. The photographs were of Meera with another man, intimate and personal, and the letter was a heartfelt note from the same man, reminiscing about their past and expressing a longing to reconnect. The discovery was like a punch to Raj's gut, a painful jolt that brought a flood of questions and doubts.

Confronting Meera was not easy, but it was inevitable. "Who is this person, Meera? Why have you never mentioned him?" Raj's voice was a mix of hurt and disbelief as he confronted her with the envelope in hand.

Meera, visibly shaken by the revelation, struggled to explain. "He's someone from my past, before we met. I thought it was over, but he reached out again. I didn't know how to tell you."

The conversation that followed was a tumultuous one, filled with accusations, tears, and a profound sense of betrayal. For Raj, it wasn't just the existence of someone from Meera's past; it was the secrecy and the apparent emotional connection that still lingered, which left him feeling betrayed.

This revelation uncovered more than just a secret; it laid bare the vulnerabilities and trust issues in their marriage. Meera's concealment of her past relationship and the recent reconnection with this person magnified the already existing cracks in their relationship.

In the muted light of their bedroom, Raj and Meera sat in heavy silence, the air between them charged with hurt and disbelief. Raj, with the envelope still in his hand, felt a chasm open up inside him, a mix of betrayal and heartbreak.

"Meera, how could you keep this from me? How long has this been going on?" Raj's voice trembled, each word heavy with pain.

Meera, her eyes brimming with tears, responded in a voice choked with emotion. "Raj, it's not what it looks like. I never meant to betray you. He was a part of my past, and I thought it was over."

"But it wasn't over, was it? He's still a part of your life," Raj countered, the hurt in his eyes deepening.

Meera reached out, trying to bridge the physical and emotional distance between them. "Raj, please believe me. I was going to tell you. I never intended for any of this."

Raj pulled away, the gesture widening the gap between them. "I don't know what to believe anymore, Meera. This...this changes everything."

Their conversation dwindled into a strained silence, each lost in their thoughts, grappling with the revelations and their implications. The room, once a haven of their love, now felt like a silent witness to the unraveling of their relationship.

Raj standing up and walking to the window, looking out into the night, while Meera remained seated, staring into the void that the secret had created. The night air was still, but the turmoil within them raged on, signalling a profound shift in their marriage. The trust and understanding that once defined them now seemed like distant memories, replaced by a sense of loss and uncertainty about their future together.

The Tumultuous Journey to Separation

In the heart of Mumbai, where love and dreams often intertwine, Meera and Raj found themselves caught in a whirlwind of emotional turmoil, their once cherished love now a labyrinth of pain and misunderstanding.

The revelation of Meera's hidden past was just the beginning. Their home, once a haven of affection, echoed with the silent screams of unsaid words and unshed tears. The constant advice from friends and family only deepened their wounds, turning well-meaning words into daggers of doubt and confusion.

Meera, sitting across Raj one evening, her eyes weary with fatigue, whispered, "Do you remember how we used to talk for hours? Now, we can barely look at each other." Her voice cracked, a stark reminder of the distance that had grown between them.

Raj, his gaze fixed on a fading photograph from their wedding, felt a pang of regret. "I know, Meera. We lost ourselves somewhere along the way," he admitted, the weight of his words heavy in the air.

Their decision to separate wasn't sudden. It was the culmination of weeks of sleepless nights, where the ghosts of their happier past haunted them. "Maybe some distance will help us find clarity," Raj suggested one night, his voice barely a whisper, laden with a sadness too profound to articulate.

Meera, her heart sinking, nodded in agreement. The hurt in her eyes mirrored Raj's own. "Perhaps this is the only way to save what's left of us," she replied, her voice tinged with a resignation that spoke volumes.

The process of separation was gruelling. The days leading up to their mutual decision were filled with an agonizing re-evaluation of their relationship. Each conversation, each memory revisited, was a reminder of the love that had once bound them tightly, now unravelling thread by thread.

As they sat in the lawyer's office, signing the papers that marked the end of their marital bond, a sombre realization dawned upon them. This wasn't just the end of their marriage; it was the end of a dream they had nurtured together. The finality of their signatures was a silent testament to the love that had once flourished, now relegated to the annals of their memories.

Walking out of the office, they exchanged a final, lingering glance. It wasn't laced with bitterness or resentment, but with a profound sadness for the loss of a relationship that was once the center of their world.

On this poignant note, capturing the heartache and emotional turbulence of Meera and Raj's journey towards separation. Their path, fraught with pain and introspection, reflects the complexities of love and the often-painful journey towards letting go.

In the bustling city of Mumbai, under the vast canopy of the starlit sky, Meera and Raj stepped into a future apart, their hearts heavy with the memories of a love that once was, and the painful acceptance of a love that could no longer be.

The Heartrending Farewell

In the wake of their harrowing decision to part ways, Meera and Raj found themselves adrift in a sea of emotions, their hearts torn between the love they once shared and the painful reality of their present. The streets of Mumbai, once a canvas of their shared dreams, now echoed with the silent whispers of their sorrow.

Meera, returning to her mother's house, felt the weight of societal gaze, each look a piercing reminder of her impending divorce. The whispered judgments and the pitying glances were like invisible shackles, reminding her of the societal stigma attached to a separated woman in India. In the solitude of her old room, Meera grappled with a torrent of emotions – the fear of an uncertain future, the anguish of lost love, and the suffocating pressure of societal norms.

Raj, on the other hand, found himself confronting a different battle. The emptiness of their shared apartment was a constant reminder of Meera's absence. His family's attempts at consolation often felt like subtle reproaches, their disappointment in the failed marriage a silent echo in every sympathetic word. The burden of societal expectations weighed heavily on him, each family gathering a reminder of his perceived failure as a husband.

As they embarked on the legal proceedings for a mutual consent divorce, the reality of their situation hit them with renewed force. The court visits were a stark departure from the life they had envisioned, each session a labyrinth of legalities and emotional upheaval.

Meera sat outside the courtroom, her eyes tracing the patterns on the floor, lost in thoughts. The journey from being a beloved wife to a petitioner in a divorce case was heart-wrenching. "How did we come to this, Raj?" she murmured during one of their silent waits, her voice barely a whisper, laden with despair.

Raj, sitting beside her, felt a lump in his throat. "I wish I knew, Meera. I wish things were different," he replied, his words heavy with regret.

Their conversations, once filled with laughter and dreams, were now reduced to terse exchanges, punctuated by long silences. The final hearing was a somber affair; the judge's words declaring their marriage dissolved were like a final nail in the coffin of their relationship.

Walking out of the courtroom, Meera and Raj shared a final, lingering glance, not just at each other, but at the remnants of a life they once cherished. The air around them was thick with unspoken words and unshed tears.

On this somber note, encapsulating the profound pain and emotional turmoil of Meera and Raj's separation. Their journey, a poignant testament to the challenges faced by couples in Indian society, highlights the complexities of love, marriage, and the societal intricacies of divorce.

In the heart of Mumbai, under the watchful eyes of a society bound by tradition and expectations, Meera and Raj stepped into a world unknown, their hearts heavy with the memories of a love that once promised forever, now lost in the echoes of time.

Closure: Echoes of a Lost Forever

As the chapter draws to its close, Meera and Raj stand at a poignant crossroads, their hearts laden with the echoes of a love that once blossomed in the vibrant heart of Mumbai, now withering in the silent throes of separation. The city, a mute spectator to their unravelling saga, resonates with the unspoken grief and unfulfilled promises of their relationship.

In the narrow, bustling lanes of Mumbai, where their love story once danced to the rhythm of rain and laughter, Meera now walks alone. Each step is heavy with a sense of loss, the sights and sounds of the city a stark reminder of what could have been. The comfort of her mother's home offers little solace, as the whispers of society weave a complex web of sympathy and judgment around her.

Raj, amidst the solitude of the home they once shared, grapples with an overwhelming sense of emptiness. The walls echo with the remnants of their shared dreams and aspirations, now fading memories in the vast void of his heart. His family's well-meaning concern does little to ease the burden of societal expectations and his own inner turmoil.

The finality of the court's decree, severing the bonds of their marriage, leaves them adrift in a sea of uncertainty and introspection. The mutual consent divorce, a decision taken in the hope of a less painful closure, brings little relief from the anguish of their fractured dreams.

As they step out of the courtroom for the last time, a final glance exchanged between them speaks volumes. It is a look that conveys the depth of their shared journey, a silent acknowledgment of the love that once was, and the pain of its dissolution. It's a farewell not just to each other, but to the life they had envisioned together.

A tapestry of poignant emotions, painting a vivid picture of the heartache and complexity that entangles modern love and marriage in the societal fabric of India. Meera and Raj, once bound by the promise of forever, now tread separate paths, their love story etched in the annals of time, a bittersweet symphony of love, loss, and life's unending quest for happiness.

Echoes of the Past

In the quiet aftermath of their divorce, Meera and Raj each wandered down their solitary paths, the echoes of their shared past resonating in the silence of their new lives. The journey was not just a path to healing but a poignant reflection on what had once been.

Meera found solace in the familiar streets of Mumbai, her steps often leading her to places drenched in memories of Raj. Strolling along Marine Drive, the sight of couples walking hand in hand would sometimes catch her off guard, triggering a cascade of recollections. She would remember the laughter they shared, the dreams they wove as they gazed at the endless sea. These memories, once a source of heartache, gradually morphed into bittersweet reminiscences, a silent acknowledgment of the love that had once flourished.

Raj's journey, too, was tinged with reflections of Meera. In the solitude of his kitchen, where he found refuge in the art of cooking, certain flavors and aromas would transport him back to moments shared with Meera. The taste of a particular spice, the texture of a dish they once cooked together – each was a reminder of a time when love, not sorrow, was the ingredient that bound them. Though these memories brought a pang of longing, they also reminded him of the joy they had once found in each other's company.

The nights were particularly reflective for both Meera and Raj. In the silence of her apartment, Meera would often find herself gazing at the stars, wondering if Raj was looking at the same sky. Those starlit nights were once theirs, filled with plans for a future that now lay in fragments.

For Raj, evenings were a time of introspection. The quiet of his home, once filled with Meera's presence, echoed with the laughter and conversations now confined to memories. He would sit on his balcony, looking out over the city they once dreamed of conquering together, feeling a mix of loss and gratitude.

Social gatherings, too, became moments of silent reflection. Meera, surrounded by friends, would sometimes find her mind drifting to the times when Raj was her plus one. The sense of his absence was palpable, a void that friends, no matter how caring, couldn't fill.

Raj, in moments of family celebrations, would catch himself scanning the room, momentarily forgetting that Meera would no longer be there, smiling at him from across the room. These realizations, though brief, were sharp reminders of their separate realities.

As time passed, the sharpness of their loss dulled into a soft ache, a reminder of a love that had been beautiful in its existence and poignant in its departure. Meera and Raj, in their own ways, learned to embrace the solitude, finding strength in the memories that once pained them.

In the wake of their divorce, Meera and Raj faced a reality starkly different from their lives as a married couple or as single individuals before that. Their new existence brought with it a myriad of emotions and societal perceptions that neither had anticipated.

For Meera, returning to her mother's house as a divorced woman brought a unique set of challenges. The way people in her family and society looked at her had changed; there was an unspoken pity in their eyes, a silent judgment that weighed heavily on her. The once vibrant and independent Meera found herself grappling with a sense of failure, her confidence eroded by the whispers and stares of those around her. She faced the world with a forced smile, but inside, the battle with her self-esteem raged on.

Raj's experience was no less challenging. At work and in his social circles, he sensed a shift in how people interacted with him. There was an awkwardness, a hesitation, as if his divorce was a contagious malady best kept at a distance. This change in perception left him feeling isolated, his self-assurance diminishing with each passing day.

The loss of their partnership was another blow. Both Meera and Raj felt the void of each other's presence acutely. The companionship and love that had once been their anchor were now replaced by a loneliness that lingered in their respective homes. Memories of shared laughter and dreams would often surface unbidden, leaving them adrift in a sea of what-ifs and regrets.

Raj, in particular, found the emotional toll of the divorce overwhelming. The once cheerful and enthusiastic chef found himself battling anxiety and depression, his mental health deteriorating as he struggled to come to terms with his new reality. He eventually sought professional help, turning to counseling and medication to navigate the turbulent waters of his psyche. The journey towards recovery was slow and arduous, each day a small step towards regaining his lost peace of mind.

Their conversations, once filled with plans for the future and intimate moments, were now limited to occasional, necessary exchanges, each interaction a reminder of the chasm that had grown between them. The ease and warmth that once defined their communication were replaced by a formal politeness, a barrier neither knew how to breach.

As Meera and Raj journeyed through this labyrinth of post-divorce life, they each faced their own battles – battles of societal perception, personal demons, and the haunting question of where they belonged in a world that seemed to view them through a different lens.

The journey through the aftermath of their divorce was akin to navigating a dense fog for Meera and Raj. Each day brought with it a new challenge, a new reminder of the life they had once envisioned together but was now just a collage of memories, both bitter and sweet.

Meera's return to her parental home was a retreat but not a sanctuary. The house, once a place of unconditional love and support, now felt like a hall of mirrors reflecting her 'failed' marital status from every angle. Conversations at family gatherings, once lively and inclusive, now often skirted around her, as if her divorce was an uncomfortable truth best left unacknowledged. The sympathetic glances from relatives felt like veiled judgments, making her feel more like an outsider than a beloved daughter. The societal lens through which she was now viewed seemed to magnify her every move, adding a layer of self-consciousness to her once carefree spirit.

Raj's world, too, had turned upside down. The camaraderie he once shared with his colleagues and friends seemed to have evaporated overnight. His presence was now often met with an uneasy silence or forced conversations. The divide was not blatant, but it was there – a subtle yet unmistakable change in attitudes that left him feeling isolated in a crowd. His professional life, once a source of pride and joy, now felt like walking on a tightrope, balancing his personal turmoil with his professional responsibilities.

The void left by their partnership was profound. The house they once shared, now just Raj's abode, echoed with the silence of Meera's absence. Each corner, each artifact, was a reminder of a dream unfulfilled. For Raj, the silence was deafening, each tick of the clock a reminder of the gaping hole in his life. The loneliness was a constant companion, only to be drowned out by the clatter of pots and pans as he sought refuge in his cooking – a bittersweet escape that brought temporary solace but also poignant reminders of Meera's absence.

For Meera, the struggle was no less significant. Her professional achievements, though fulfilling, could not fill the emptiness that lingered in her heart. The independence she had once cherished now felt like a cold comfort. Her walks along Marine Drive, once a shared ritual, were now solitary reflections – a time to piece together her fragmented self-esteem and to face the reality of her new life.

As months passed, the sharpness of their pain dulled to a persistent ache, a constant undercurrent in their daily lives. But amidst this turmoil, there were moments of clarity and acceptance. Small victories in their personal and professional lives began to pave the way for healing. They learned to find solace in their solitude, to appreciate the quiet moments of introspection that their new lives afforded them.

Meera and Raj beginning to embrace their individual journeys. Though the path was lined with the shadows of their past, they also found spots of light – moments of self-realization, of acceptance, and of hope. These flickers of light were reminders that even in the darkest of times, the human spirit can find ways to heal and grow. In their own separate ways, Meera and Raj were learning to navigate through the shadows, moving towards a future where the pain of the past was a memory, not a daily reality.

A Chance Reunion in Shadows of Past

In the ensuing months post-divorce, Meera and Raj embarked on their solitary paths, grappling with the aftermath of their split. The echoes of their shared past reverberated in their lives, shaping their days in subtle yet profound ways.

Amidst this journey of rediscovery, serendipity played its hand, orchestrating a chance encounter that brought them face to face once again. It was at an art exhibition in the bustling heart of Mumbai, a setting that resonated with their shared love for the arts, where destiny decided to intertwine their paths once more.

The encounter was unexpected, stirring a whirlwind of emotions. The initial awkwardness quickly gave way to a hesitant but genuine conversation, a far cry from the strained exchanges of their final days together.

Meera, summoning her courage, broke the ice. "Raj, I never wanted it to end the way it did," she began, her voice laced with a sorrow that had matured over time. "I never meant to hurt you. My past... it was just that, the past."

Raj, his expression a mix of surprise and contemplation, listened intently. The wounds of the past were still tender, but time had lent him a perspective that was absent before. "I know, Meera. I've had a lot of time to think. We both made mistakes. Perhaps we were just not meant to be, at least not in the way we thought."

Their conversation meandered through the lanes of their shared memories, each recollection a bittersweet reminder of what they had lost and also what they had gained. Laughter came easier now, tinged with a sense of nostalgia, free from the bitterness that once enveloped their interactions.

As the evening waned, they found themselves at a crossroads – not as lovers but as two individuals who had shared a significant journey. "It's odd, isn't it? How we've come full circle," Meera mused, a hint of wistfulness in her tone.

Raj nodded, "Life is unpredictable. But I'm glad we met again, Meera. As friends, with no regrets, just respect for what we had and what we've become."

Their parting that evening was not a goodbye but a gentle acknowledgment of a new beginning – a friendship born from the ashes of their past. It was a testament to their growth and the enduring respect they held for each other.

As they walked away from the exhibition, the Mumbai night sky aglow with stars, Meera and Raj carried with them a sense of closure, a feeling of peace that had eluded them in the tumultuous days of their divorce.

Their chance reunion, under the canopy of art and shared memories, had offered them a rare opportunity – to reconcile with their past, to acknowledge their growth, and to appreciate the intricate tapestry of life's experiences.

In the labyrinth of their emotions, as Meera and Raj parted ways after their unexpected reunion, they each carried a bittersweet symphony of feelings. The encounter was a poignant reminder of the love they once shared, a love that had morphed into a deep, abiding respect born from the ashes of their shared past.

Meera walked back to her car, her heart heavy yet strangely light. The meeting had reopened old wounds, but it had also brought a sense of closure. The pain of their divorce had been a dark cloud in her life, casting a shadow over her every day. But in speaking to Raj again, she realized the strength she had garnered from their separation. It was a painful, yet necessary chapter in her life, one that taught her resilience and the value of self-love.

Raj, standing alone amidst the dwindling crowd, felt a similar cascade of emotions. The shock and hurt from their divorce had shaken him to his core, leading him down a path of introspection and personal growth. Seeing Meera again had initially reopened old fears and insecurities, but their conversation reminded him of the beautiful moments they had shared. It was a revelation that even in pain, there was learning and an opportunity for emotional healing.

Their conversation, filled with shared memories and acknowledgments of past mistakes, was a cathartic experience. It was a recognition that while their journey as a couple had ended, the journey of personal growth and understanding continued. The hurt and love they had experienced were not in vain; they were integral to the individuals they had become.

As they both drove away into the Mumbai night, the city lights flickering like distant stars, there was a silent acknowledgment between them. A realization that sometimes, love doesn't end in the way one expects. It transforms, evolves, and sometimes, it leads to unexpected friendships. It was a testament to their maturity and the unspoken respect they still harboured for each other.

On a note of reflective tranquillity, with Meera and Raj moving forward in their lives, enriched by the lessons of their past. They had learned that love, in its many forms, is a journey not just of the heart, but of the soul – a journey that teaches, hurts, heals, and ultimately, transforms.

New Horizons

The city of Mumbai, ever vibrant and pulsing with life, witnessed the unfolding of a new chapter for Meera and Raj. Their chance encounter had been a bridge between their shared past and their individual futures, leaving them with a renewed sense of purpose.

Meera: A Journey of Self-Rediscovery

Meera's life, post their serendipitous reunion, took on a vibrant hue. She poured her soul into her architectural designs, each line and curve a testament to her growth and resilience. The once familiar lanes of Mumbai now revealed new facets, reflecting her journey of self-discovery. Her weekends were spent in art galleries and dance studios, embracing the joy of self-expression that she had long denied herself.

Her evenings were often spent on her balcony, gazing at the stars that had silently witnessed her transformation. They were no longer just celestial bodies but symbols of hope and the infinite possibilities that lay ahead. The pain of her past, while still a part of her, had transformed into a source of strength, propelling her forward on her path of independence and self-realization.

Raj: Embracing New Beginnings

Raj, on the other hand, found a renewed passion in his culinary endeavors. His restaurant had become more than just a place of business; it was a canvas for his creativity and a haven for his dreams. He experimented with new flavors and techniques, each dish a celebration of his journey from the shadows of his past.

His interactions with customers and staff were imbued with a genuine warmth, a reflection of the peace he had found. The restaurant's success was not just a professional achievement but a personal triumph over the trials he had faced. On quiet nights, he would walk along the shores of Juhu Beach, the rhythmic sound of the waves echoing the calmness that had settled in his heart. His path, though solitary, was filled with the contentment of self-discovery and the excitement of new beginnings.

Intersecting Paths in Separate Journeys

Though their lives had diverged, the city occasionally brought Meera and Raj into each other's orbit. A fleeting glance across a busy street, a polite nod in a crowded café – these brief encounters were no longer tinged with sadness but with mutual respect and a shared understanding of their respective journeys.

Their paths, enriched by their past experiences, continued to unfold in parallel narratives. They were reminders that life, in its infinite complexity, is a mosaic of encounters and experiences, each playing a crucial role in shaping one's destiny.

As they navigated through their separate lives, the lessons of love, resilience, and transformation they had learned together remained with them, guiding lights in their continuous journey of growth and self-discovery. In the heart of Mumbai, Meera and Raj walked their paths – separate yet connected, distinct yet intertwined, each a testament to the enduring power of the human spirit.

The Whispers of Heart and Soul

In the bustling heart of Mumbai, Meera and Raj, though apart, traverse their individual journeys, their paths entwined with memories and personal growth. Chapter 15 delicately unfolds their stories, tinged with moments of introspection and emotional revelations.

Meera's Heartfelt Journey:

Meera, amidst the solitude of the majestic Himalayas, finds herself in an emotional embrace with nature. This solo trip, more than an escape, becomes a pilgrimage to the depths of her soul. As she treks through the verdant trails, each step resonates with a newfound understanding of herself. The cool mountain breeze whispers echoes of her past, each gust a reminder of the love she shared with Raj. One evening, as she watches the sunset paint the sky in hues of fiery orange and calming purple, a surge of emotions overflows. It's here, in the embrace of the Himalayan twilight, that she sheds tears for what was lost, allowing her heart to start healing.

Back in Mumbai, her career scales new heights with her latest architectural venture. But it's more than professional success – it's a triumph of her spirit. The night her project receives acclaim, she stands on the stage, her heart swelling with pride and a poignant ache. In the crowd, she imagines Raj's smiling face, silently sharing her success. This bittersweet moment is a testament to her resilience and the enduring impact of their shared journey.

Raj's Path of Reflection:

Raj finds solace in the quiet corners of his restaurant after hours. One evening, as he experiments with a new recipe, a familiar tune plays on the radio – a melody that he and Meera once danced to in their living room. The memories flood back, each note a reminder of their laughter, their dreams, their shared life. Standing alone in his kitchen, Raj allows himself a moment of vulnerability, letting the music wash over him, acknowledging the love that once was.

Embracing mindfulness, Raj discovers the power of self-reflection. Each session of meditation brings him closer to understanding the intertwining of love and loss. In the serenity of his thoughts, he learns to forgive – not just Meera, but also himself, for the dreams that turned to dust. This journey of forgiveness is his pathway to peace, a balm for the soul that still cares deeply for the love that shaped him.

Independent Yet Connected:

Through these personal endeavours, Meera and Raj learned to embrace their solitude, finding joy and fulfilment in their passions. Their journey of self-discovery was not just about moving on from their past but about building a future where they were complete within themselves.

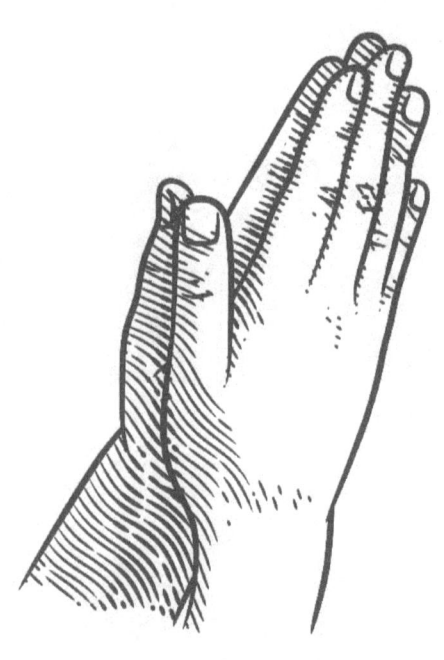

The Art of Letting Go

In the heart of Mumbai's bustling energy, amidst a backdrop of art and creativity, Meera and Raj found themselves embarking on a poignant journey of closure. A serendipitous encounter at an art exhibition paved the way for a transformative conversation, one that would gently untangle the lingering threads of their shared past.

Encounter at the Exhibition:

The air was thick with the scent of oil paints and the subtle buzz of cultured voices discussing art. Meera, immersed in the vibrant hues of a canvas, felt a familiar presence beside her. Turning, she found herself facing Raj, his appearance a stark reminder of a shared history now behind them.

"Raj, this is unexpected," Meera said, her voice a mixture of surprise and calm acceptance.

"Life is full of unexpected turns, isn't it?" Raj replied, his eyes meeting hers with a knowing look.

The Conversation Unfolds:

They navigated through the crowds to a quieter spot, a little cocoon amidst the chaos, where their conversation could unfold with honesty and reflection.

"Seeing all this art, it reminds me of us. Our story was a tapestry of so many emotions, wasn't it?" Meera started, her gaze drifting back to the art.

"It was," Raj agreed. "And like any piece of art, it had its imperfections, its unfinished edges."

Delving into Forgiveness:

Meera's eyes met Raj's, a depth of understanding passing between them. "I've been learning, Raj, learning about the art of letting go. I forgive you, and more importantly, I forgive myself."

Raj's response was laced with introspection. "Forgiveness... it's a powerful thing. It's freeing, isn't it? I too have come to terms with our past. Our story had its time, and now it's time to turn the page."

Sharing Personal Growth:

Their conversation meandered through the landscapes of their individual journeys since parting ways. Meera spoke of her architectural projects, how they mirrored her path of healing and self-discovery. Raj shared tales from his café, each new recipe a testament to his journey of self-improvement.

Embracing Closure:

As the evening light faded, their conversation reached a natural, peaceful conclusion. There was no dramatic goodbye, no tears, just a mutual understanding that they were both moving forward, separately but stronger.

"I'm glad we met tonight, Raj. It feels like we've finally closed a long-open door," Meera said, a note of finality in her voice.

"And behind that door lies new beginnings for us both," Raj added, a sense of hope coloring his words.

Parting on a New Note:

As they parted ways, the weight of unsaid words and unresolved emotions had lifted. They had not just conversed but had connected on a level that transcended their past love, a connection rooted in mutual respect and understanding.

Their steps away from each other were not steps of separation, but strides towards their individual futures, illuminated by the art of letting go and the grace of forgiveness. Their shared history remained a part of them, but now as a chapter concluded with wisdom and serenity.

Paths of Rediscovery

In the vibrant city of Mumbai, Meera and Raj embarked on parallel journeys of self-discovery. Their chance encounter had sparked a newfound appreciation for their individual paths, illuminating the importance of personal growth and independence.

Meera: Embracing Independence:

Meera found herself immersed in her architectural projects, each design more daring and innovative than the last. She was often seen at construction sites, her eyes sparkling with the same passion that once lit up her conversations with Raj. Her projects weren't just buildings; they were manifestations of her journey, structures that stood tall and proud, much like her.

One evening, while presenting a new project, she found herself recounting a memory of Raj. "He always encouraged me to push my boundaries," she shared with a colleague, her voice tinged with gratitude. It was a moment of acknowledgment, an understanding that her past with Raj was an integral part of her present growth.

Raj: Culinary Ventures and Self-Reflection:

Raj, meanwhile, poured his soul into his café. He introduced a series of 'experimental nights', where patrons could experience his culinary innovations. Each dish told a story, some subtly reflecting his journey post-divorce.

During one such night, as he explained the inspiration behind a particularly intricate dish, he found himself sharing insights from his marriage with Meera. "Our experiences, good and bad, shape us," he mused to a table of attentive listeners. In these moments of sharing, Raj found a therapeutic release, a way to channel his reflections into something beautiful and tangible.

Individual Growth and Public Recognition:

Their individual pursuits did not go unnoticed. Meera received an award for her innovative architectural designs, a recognition that filled her with a sense of accomplishment and pride. Raj's café began to gain popularity, not just for its food but also as a space where stories and experiences were woven into the fabric of dining.

A Moment of Reflection:

One particular evening, as Meera stood on her balcony, looking out over the city that had seen her rise, fall, and rise again, she realized how far she had come. The city lights shimmered like distant stars, each a reminder of a challenge overcome, a dream realized.

Across town, Raj closed his café for the night, a sense of contentment in his heart. He had turned his once shared dream with Meera into a personal triumph, a place that resonated with his journey of self-discovery.

Serendipitous Reencounter at the Book Café

In the heart of Mumbai, amidst the hum of the bustling city, a quaint book café in Bandra sets the stage for an unexpected reunion. The café, a sanctuary of tranquility and nostalgia, becomes the backdrop for Meera and Raj's serendipitous encounter, echoing their first meeting years ago.

A Familiar Setting:

As Meera steps into the café, the familiar scent of coffee and old books envelops her, transporting her back in time. She finds her favorite spot by the window, the same place where she first met Raj. Lost in a book, she's unaware of his presence until a gentle voice interrupts her thoughts.

"Is the book as captivating as the first time we met?" Raj stands there, a smile playing on his lips, mirroring the day they first crossed paths.

Meera looks up, surprised and momentarily speechless. The years seem to melt away as she returns his smile. "It's an old favorite," she replies, her heart fluttering with a mix of nostalgia and excitement.

Rekindling Conversations:

Their conversation flows effortlessly, as if the years apart have only been a brief pause. They talk about everything from their favorite authors to the turns their lives have taken since their divorce. The café's cozy ambiance, with its soft lighting and the quiet murmur of other patrons, lends a sense of intimacy to their reunion.

As they chat, laughter and shared memories fill the air, bridging the gap time has created. They reminisce about their past, but more importantly, they talk about their individual journeys of growth and self-discovery. The ease of their interaction is a testament to the enduring bond they share, a bond that has evolved yet remains deeply rooted.

An Unspoken Connection:

As they delve deeper into conversation, the connection they once shared flickers back to life. It's different now, tempered by experience and personal growth, but the underlying affection and mutual respect are unmistakable.

The café begins to empty as the evening progresses, but Meera and Raj are lost in their world, the world they once shared and are now rediscovering. The realization that they still enjoy each other's company is a revelation, bringing with it a sense of comfort and familiarity.

Closure and Continuation:

Finally, as the night draws in, they prepare to part ways. Raj hesitates before speaking, "Meera, would you be open to meeting again? As friends, to share more of these moments?"

Meera's response comes with a warmth that lights up her eyes. "I would like that, Raj. There's still so much we haven't spoken about."

Their goodbye is warm and lingering, a stark contrast to the cold farewells of their past. As they step out of the café, the cool Mumbai breeze carries with it a sense of new beginnings. They walk away, not as estranged ex-partners but as two individuals on a journey of rediscovery, both of themselves and of the connection they share.

The story of Meera and Raj takes a hopeful turn, symbolizing the power of time, healing, and the enduring nature of true connections. Their journey continues, paralleled yet intertwined, a testament to the resilience of the human spirit and the transformative power of life's unexpected encounters.

Rekindled Bonds and New Beginnings

After their serendipitous meeting at the café, Meera and Raj find themselves drawn into a series of encounters, each marked by a sense of ease and rediscovery. Their relationship, once fraught with the complexities of marriage and the pain of divorce, now takes on a new dimension, colored by their individual growth and the passage of time.

Rediscovery Through Shared Interests:

Meera invites Raj to a photography exhibition, knowing his newfound passion for capturing moments. As they wander through the gallery, discussing the art, there's a harmony in their perspectives, a reflection of the understanding they've always shared. Raj, in turn, invites Meera to a culinary workshop at his restaurant, engaging her in the world of flavors and aromas that he has come to love. These shared experiences bring them closer, allowing them to appreciate the individuals they have become.

Conversations of Depth and Maturity:

Their meetings are often filled with conversations that dive deep into their aspirations, fears, and the lessons learned from their past. They talk about their divorce, not with bitterness, but with a maturity that comes from acceptance and healing. This open communication becomes a bridge, reconnecting them in a way that is profound yet devoid of past resentments.

A Friendship Blossoms:

What starts as casual meetings soon blossoms into a comfortable friendship. They find joy in each other's company, a joy that is untainted by the complexities of their previous relationship. This newfound friendship is a safe space where they can be themselves without the pressures and expectations that once strained their marriage.

Acknowledging the Past, Embracing the Present:

One evening, as they sit by the seafront at Marine Drive, Meera turns to Raj and says, "It's strange how life brings us full circle. I'm grateful for our past; it's brought us here, as friends."

Raj nods in agreement, "Our journey had its share of storms, but look where we are now. I cherish what we have now, Meera."

A Future of Possibilities:

As they continue to spend time together, the boundaries of friendship subtly blur, leaving them in a space that is familiar yet new. The comfort of their interactions, the laughter, and the shared silences hint at an underlying possibility of something more.

However, both Meera and Raj are conscious of the journey they have been through. They choose to take things slow, allowing their relationship to evolve naturally, without the rush and intensity that once defined their younger selves.

Meera and Raj are seen walking away from the seafront, their laughter mingling with the Mumbai night. The city, with its vibrant energy and endless possibilities, mirrors their own state of being - hopeful, content, and open to the new chapters of life that await them.

Their story, a testament to the unpredictability of life and the enduring nature of true connections, continues to unfold, marked by a newfound appreciation for each other and the journey they have shared.

Reunion Amidst Reservations

A Fateful Conversation at Their Old Haunt

In the quaint café that once witnessed the beginning of their story, Meera and Raj sat across from each other, enveloped in a familiar yet distant atmosphere. The air was thick with unspoken words and memories.

Meera, her eyes reflecting the café's soft lighting, broke the silence. "Raj, have you ever thought about... us? About giving us another chance?"

Raj's gaze, intense and thoughtful, met hers. "Every single day, Meera. But stepping back into that world... it's daunting, not just for us, but thinking of my family, the society..."

Their conversation spiralled into the depths of their fears and hopes, a delicate dance of emotions, testing the waters of a decision that could redefine their lives.

Deciding to Face the Future Together

Days passed, each filled with contemplation and subtle affirmations. The decision to remarry, they knew, was laden with complexities far beyond their personal realm.

Sitting together in Raj's apartment, the city's night sky a canvas of their shared uncertainties, Raj voiced his concerns, "The societal backlash, the whispers, the judgmental stares... Can we endure that again, Meera?"

Meera, her hand gently squeezing his, reassured him, "The thought of facing life's turbulence without you is far more daunting, Raj. We have grown, healed, and emerged stronger. We owe ourselves this chance."

Their resolve, though flickering, remained undeterred, a promise to each other that they were ready to face the impending storms together.

Facing Their Families:

The meeting with their families was a maelstrom of emotions. Meera, with no parents of her own and only a stepmother who was distant at best, felt a deep-seated anxiety. Raj, on his part, grappled with the absence of his late father and the apprehensions of his family.

"You're walking back into a labyrinth," Meera's stepmother remarked, her tone sceptical.

Raj's mother added, her voice laced with concern, "The societal judgments, the talk behind your backs... Are you prepared for all that again?"

Despite the palpable tension, Meera and Raj stood united. "We understand your worries," Meera said firmly, "but we've learned from our past. Our decision is not impulsive but a step towards a future we both desire and deserve."

The families, though reluctant, began to sense the conviction and mutual respect in their decision. It was a reluctant admission that perhaps, against all odds, their love could indeed turn a new leaf.

Embracing What Lies Ahead

As they stepped out into the Mumbai night, the weight of their decision pressed heavily on them. The path to remarrying was strewn not just with personal challenges but societal barriers and familial concerns.

Raj, his hand firmly clasped in Meera's, whispered against the hum of the city, "As long as we're together, we can brave any storm."

Meera, her eyes reflecting the resolve in her heart, nodded. "Together, we'll transform these challenges into the foundations of our new beginning."

Hand in hand, they walked through the streets, under the watchful gaze of the stars. Their love, once lost in the turmoil of life, now sought a new horizon – a testament to their belief in each other and the enduring power of a love that had weathered life's trials, ready to be 'Married but Happily Single'.

The Second Wedding - A Bold Statement

Late Night Conversation in Raj's Living Room

Meera and Raj sat in his living room, a nervous energy filling the space. The clock ticked loudly in the background, marking the silence that stretched between them.

Raj broke the silence, his voice hesitant, "Meera, are we ready for this? To face everyone again... together?"

Meera looked up, her eyes reflecting a mix of resolve and apprehension. "We have to be, Raj. This isn't just about us. It's about proving to everyone that what we have is worth fighting for."

They knew the path ahead was fraught with whispers and judgments. But in that room, a decision was made – a court marriage, simple yet powerful in its message.

The Day of the Court Marriage

The morning air was crisp as Meera and Raj made their way to the registrar's office. There was a solemnity to their steps, a deep awareness of the gravity of this step. Clad in simple yet elegant attire, they both understood the symbolism of this day – it wasn't just a marriage ceremony, it was a reclamation of their love, a declaration that they had endured the storm and emerged together.

As they entered the registrar's office, their hands found each other, an unspoken communication of support and love. The office was stark, devoid of the usual celebratory trappings of a wedding, yet for them, it was a shrine of their commitment.

Standing before the registrar, Meera's heart fluttered with a blend of nervousness and joy. This moment was a poignant reminder of their first wedding, yet so different. It was devoid of naivety, enriched instead with the wisdom of their experiences.

Raj gazed into Meera's eyes as they exchanged vows. These words had a profound depth now, forged in the fires of their separation and reunion. Their voices were steady, brimming with emotion as they vowed to stand by each other, come what may.

The signing of the register was a quiet affair, their signatures intertwining as a testament to their unbroken bond, a bond that had been tested and had triumphed.

Returning to Raj's Neighbourhood

The walk back to Raj's neighbourhood was a journey filled with mixed emotions. Meera felt a surge of pride holding Raj's hand, yet there was an undercurrent of apprehension about the neighbours' reactions.

As they entered the familiar streets, curious glances and hushed whispers greeted them. Meera felt a momentary pang of vulnerability, the weight of their stares a reminder of the societal hurdles they had chosen to face.

Raj, sensing her discomfort, squeezed her hand reassuringly. "Remember, we're in this together," he whispered, his voice a pillar of strength.

A neighbour, cloaked in the guise of concern, approached them with veiled judgments thinly disguised as congratulations. Meera felt a momentary flicker of anger, but Raj's calm demeanour steadied her. They faced the encounter with dignity, their responses polite yet firm, a clear message that their decision was theirs alone to make and understand.

As they continued their walk, Meera's initial unease transformed into a sense of empowerment. Each step was a defiance, a statement that their love was their own, unbounded by societal norms.

Encountering Judgment

The following days tested their resolve. One evening, while taking a walk, they overheard a neighbor's harsh comment. Meera's steps faltered, tears brimming in her eyes.

Raj stopped, turning to face her. "Meera, look at me. We don't need their validation. Our love, our decision to be together again – that's what matters."

Meera nodded, drawing strength from his words. Together, they continued their walk, a silent rebellion against the judgmental whispers.

In the Privacy of Their Home

That night, in the sanctuary of Raj's home, now theirs again, they reflected on the day. There were no grand celebrations, just the two of them, yet it felt more meaningful than any lavish ceremony could have been.

They talked late into the night, sharing their dreams and aspirations for the future. This second marriage was not just a new chapter in their love story; it was a testament to their resilience, to the enduring power of love over adversity.

In the quiet of their home, away from the judging eyes of the world, they found peace and strength in each other's presence. Their second marriage, marked by simplicity and profound love, was a bold statement to the world – a declaration that their love was unbreakable, a phoenix risen from the ashes of societal norms and expectations.

Building an Empire – A Culinary and Design Odyssey

The Onset: Navigating the Social Labyrinth

Two years into their reunion, the initial turbulence of Meera moving back in with Raj had settled into a quieter, albeit still present, hum of neighbourhood gossip. In a significant gathering at their local community centre, the couple faced the remnants of societal scepticism.

As they interacted with neighbours, Mrs. Sharma, a long-time resident, cautiously broached the subject, "It's quite a story, you two getting back together. Most unusual..."

Raj, with a supportive glance towards Meera, replied confidently, "Life often writes the most unexpected stories. We're just glad ours had a happy continuation." Meera, with a warm yet firm tone, added, "And we're grateful for the understanding we've received from everyone."

Their response was met with nods, signalling a begrudging acceptance from the community. Over time, Raj's family, initially reluctant about their reunion, grew to accept Meera, seeing the undeniable bond and happiness she brought into Raj's life.

The Birth of an Idea

It was a quiet Mumbai evening, filled with the aroma of Raj's experimental cooking, when the idea that would change their lives sparked. Meera, inspired by the fusion of flavors, mused aloud, "What if we create a place where every dish tells a story, and the decor narrates Mumbai's eclectic charm?"

Raj, intrigued, added, "A culinary and design odyssey, blending our passions. It could be a unique dining experience." The excitement in his voice was palpable.

They spent hours brainstorming, with Meera sketching designs and Raj jotting down recipe ideas. Their concept for 'Indigo Fusion' was born from these sessions – a fusion of culinary art and design aesthetics.

The Launch of 'Indigo Fusion'

The launch of 'Indigo Fusion' was the culmination of months of hard work and dedication. The restaurant was a visual and gastronomic representation of their journey – vibrant, bold, and innovative.

Friends, family, and acquaintances gathered for the opening, the air buzzing with anticipation. Raj and Meera welcomed guests; their pride evident in their glowing faces. The initial apprehension from society had transformed into admiration and respect.

As diners indulged in Raj's creative dishes and admired Meera's inspired interiors, the couple received accolades and congratulations. 'Indigo Fusion' was not just a restaurant; it was a narrative of their love, resilience, and creativity.

Gradual Expansion

Encouraged by the initial success, they began considering expansion. Over the next few years, they opened new outlets across Mumbai, each carrying the essence of 'Indigo Fusion' but with unique twists reflecting the localities they were in. This gradual expansion allowed them to refine their concept and solidify their brand.

Epilogue: Realizing the Dream

Years later, Meera and Raj stood in their flagship restaurant, now a beloved spot in Mumbai. They reflected on their journey, a blend of personal and professional triumphs. Their success was not just in creating a flourishing business but in proving that their love, understanding, and shared dreams could defy societal expectations.

Their story, embodied by 'Indigo Fusion', was a narrative of resilience, creativity, and the power of partnership. It stood as a symbol of their life philosophy - 'Married but Happily Single', where togetherness and individuality coexist in harmony.

Harmony in Togetherness and Individuality

Embracing Individual Paths Within Unity

One evening, as they relaxed in their living room, Meera shared her thoughts with Raj. "I've been invited to speak at the Design Symposium in Paris next month. It's a huge opportunity, Raj."

Raj, looking up from his cookbook manuscript, smiled warmly. "That's fantastic, Meera! You must go. Your talent deserves that international stage."

Meera hesitated, "But what about 'Indigo Fusion'? And your book launch is around the same time..."

Raj reached for her hand, "We've always managed to balance our professional and personal lives. I'll handle things here. Your dreams are as important as mine."

Their conversation reflected the deep understanding and respect they had for each other's aspirations, a foundation that had strengthened their bond over the years.

A Community of Support

At a dinner party they hosted, Meera and Raj were surrounded by friends and family. The atmosphere was lively, filled with laughter and engaging conversations.

Raj's mother, joining a group, said, "Meera, the community center you designed is the talk of the town. You've brought so much pride to our family."

Meera smiled, "I couldn't have done it without your support and Raj's encouragement."

Later, as they cleared up, Raj remarked, "I love how these gatherings bring everyone together. It's like we're building a small community of our own."

Meera nodded, "Yes, a community that values individuality as much as togetherness."

A Testament to Their Philosophy

In a quiet moment together, Meera reflected on their journey. "Do you realize how far we've come, Raj? From being on the brink of losing each other to now?"

Raj looked at her thoughtfully, "It's been an incredible journey. We've learned that being married doesn't mean losing our individual selves. It's about growing together, each at our own pace, supporting each other."

Meera added, "It's about love that respects personal dreams and aspirations. We've shown that being 'Married but Happily Single' is about embracing each other's uniqueness while building a life together."

Their conversation, deep and introspective, was a testament to their evolved understanding of marriage and partnership – a balance of togetherness and individual growth.

Epilogue: Legacy and Love

The evening at Raj and Meera's home was vibrant with the chatter and laughter of family and friends gathered for a special dinner. The house, adorned with warm lights and elegant decor, resonated with a sense of joy and togetherness.

As the evening progressed, Meera glanced at Raj, a twinkle of excitement in her eyes. She had a special announcement, one that would add a new dimension to their already rich and fulfilling life.

Clapping her hands to gather everyone's attention, Meera stood up, her face glowing with an unspoken secret. The room fell silent in anticipation.

"I have a very special announcement to make," she began, her voice trembling slightly with emotion. "Raj and I are going to be parents! We're expecting our first child!"

The room erupted in cheers and applause. Raj, overwhelmed with emotion, stood up and embraced Meera, his eyes brimming with tears of joy. "This is the best surprise ever," he whispered, kissing her forehead.

Family and friends crowded around them, offering hugs and congratulations. Raj's mother, tears of happiness in her eyes, hugged Meera tightly. "You have brought us the greatest joy," she said, her voice choked with emotion.

As the evening continued, the air was filled with conversations about baby names, parenting advice, and heartfelt wishes for the couple. The excitement was palpable, a shared happiness that enveloped everyone present.

Meera, looking around at the smiling faces, felt a deep sense of contentment. This moment was more than just an announcement; it was a celebration of life, love, and the new journey they were about to embark on.

Raj, standing beside her, took her hand in his. "Our journey has been nothing short of extraordinary, and now, with our little one on the way, it's going to be even more amazing."

The night, filled with laughter and shared stories, was a beautiful testament to their life together. As the guests departed, leaving behind warm hugs and good wishes, Meera and Raj stood on their balcony, looking out at the city they loved.

In that quiet moment, under the starry Mumbai sky, they dreamt of the future. A future that held the promise of new beginnings, a continuation of their legacy of love, and the joy of bringing a new life into their world.

Their story, a narrative of overcoming challenges, embracing love, and creating a life of harmony, was an inspiration to all who knew them. In the heart of Mumbai, Meera and Raj stood together, ready for the next chapter of their lives, united in love and excited for the legacy they were about to create.

Redefining Relationships in Contemporary India

The Onset of Divorce: Understanding the Indian Context

In Indian society, the concept of divorce has traditionally been stigmatized, considered a failure of not just the individuals involved but their families as well. However, with changing societal norms, economic empowerment, and a growing emphasis on individual well-being, the landscape is evolving.

In urban areas, especially, couples like Meera and Raj are increasingly viewing divorce not as a social taboo but as a viable option in the face of irreconcilable differences. This shift is driven by several factors:

1. Rising Awareness: Greater exposure to global ideas and a better understanding of personal rights are empowering individuals to seek happiness and fulfillment.

2. Women's Empowerment: With more women entering the workforce and becoming financially independent, they are less likely to tolerate unhappy or abusive marriages.

3. Change in Family Dynamics: Joint family systems are giving way to nuclear families, reducing familial pressure to stay in an unhappy marriage.

Yet, despite these shifts, divorce in India remains a challenging journey, fraught with societal judgments and emotional upheaval.

Analysing the Causes and Solutions

1. Compatibility Issues: Often, couples find over time that their values, interests, or life goals are incompatible.

Solution: Regular communication and counselling can help bridge these gaps.

2. Financial Strains: Money problems can lead to significant stress in a marriage.

Solution: Joint financial planning and transparent discussions about money are key.

3. Extended Family Dynamics: Interference from in-laws or extended family can create tension. Solution: Setting boundaries and prioritizing the marital relationship.

4. Cultural and Religious Differences: Differences in background can become contentious.

Solution: Mutual respect and a willingness to embrace each other's cultures.

5. Infidelity: One of the most common reasons for divorce.

Solution: Building a strong foundation of trust and commitment.

6. Lack of Personal Space: Losing individual identity can harm the relationship.

Solution: Encouraging each other's personal growth and interests.

7. Communication Breakdown: Failure to communicate effectively can lead to misunderstandings. Solution: Active listening and empathy are crucial.

8. Unrealistic Expectations: Often, couples enter marriage with idealized expectations.

Solution: A realistic understanding of marriage as a partnership.

9. Domestic Abuse: Physical, emotional, or mental abuse is a serious issue.

Solution: Seeking help immediately, prioritizing personal safety.

10. Child Rearing Differences: Disagreements over parenting can create rifts.

Solution: Joint parenting strategies and shared responsibilities.

Married but Happily Single: A New Paradigm

In the extraordinary journey of Meera and Raj, the concept of 'Married but Happily Single' takes on a profound dimension. This paradigm shift challenges traditional marital expectations and offers fresh insights into the complexities millennials face today, as they navigate not only the generational gap but also the complexities of their shared past.

Understanding the Generational Divide:

The generational gap has become a significant factor contributing to divorce among millennials. Meera and Raj's story exemplifies this intricate dynamic. They are part of a generation that finds itself wedged between their parents' deeply rooted traditions, often disconnected from the digital age, and Generation Z, which effortlessly embraces technology and the internet. Millennials must act as mediators, bridging the chasm between two vastly different worlds.

Embracing a Shared Past:

One unique aspect of Meera and Raj's journey is Raj's ability to digest and reconcile with Meera's challenging past. It is a testament to his maturity and his commitment to building a future together. Raj's capacity to acknowledge and accept Meera's past, however tumultuous it may have been, is an essential part of their journey.

Raj's Transformation:

Raj's journey within the marriage is one of personal growth and resilience. He goes beyond the conventional boundaries of marriage, evolving as an individual and as a partner. His ability to forgive and embrace Meera's past is a reflection of the strength of their bond. Raj's transformation serves as a powerful example of how love, understanding, and maturity can overcome the challenges posed by a complex past.

Building a Stronger Future:

For couples facing similar situations, Raj's experience offers a beacon of hope. It illustrates that a challenging past need not define the future of a relationship. Through open communication, empathy, and a willingness to forgive, couples can move forward, hand in hand, and build a stronger, more resilient future together.

'Married but Happily Single' not only sheds light on the generational gap but also highlights the importance of acknowledging and embracing the past, however difficult it may be. It is a guide for millennials facing these complexities, offering insights into creating a marriage that celebrates both individuality and the shared experiences that shape their journey.

Concluding Thoughts: A Message of Hope and Resilience

Meera and Raj's extraordinary journey reminds us that:

Marriage is a journey of partnership, understanding, and patience.

Personal growth is vital for a healthy relationship.

Open and honest communication is the bedrock of a strong marriage.

Adaptability is essential in the face of life's changes.

Embracing individuality enriches a marriage.

A robust support system eases the challenges of marriage.

Challenging societal norms can lead to a more fulfilling relationship.

Reconciliation is possible with mutual understanding and respect.

Marriage is an evolving journey, requiring continuous commitment.

Ultimately, love, respect, and understanding can conquer even the most formidable challenges.

Understanding the Essence of Marriage: The Journey of Meera and Raj

In the intricate tapestry of life, marriage stands as one of the most profound human relationships, a bond that holds the potential to be both immensely fulfilling and challenging. It is a union that, especially in the Indian context, is often simplified to a mere 'adjustment,' a compromise of individual desires for the sake of a collective harmony. However, as the journey of Meera and Raj in 'Married but Happily Single' illustrates, marriage is far more nuanced and complex than this traditional view suggests.

The story of Meera and Raj is a poignant reflection of many Indian marriages, where the initial euphoria of love and togetherness gradually gives way to the stark realities of shared life. The critical error in their marriage, a common pitfall for many, was the oversight of an essential truth – that marriage is not just a union of two people but also a merger of two individual worlds. Each partner brings to the marriage their own dreams, aspirations, fears, and flaws. It is in the delicate balance of embracing these individual traits while nurturing the relationship where the true art of marriage lies.

In their early years, Meera and Raj found themselves lost in the whirlwind of marital responsibilities and societal expectations. The challenge was not in the everyday adjustments – the who-does-what and the what-goes-where. It was in the profound realization that in their efforts to be ideal spouses, they had inadvertently sidelined their individual identities. Their story is a testament to a common plight – where the pressure to conform to marital norms often leads to a gradual erosion of personal identity and dreams.

The turning point in their relationship came with the painful decision to separate. It was through this separation that they discovered an uncomfortable truth: their individual growth had been stunted in the shadows of their marital roles. The separation, though fraught with pain and societal stigma, became a journey of self-discovery. It allowed them to step back and reassess not just their relationship, but also their individual selves.

Their eventual decision to reunite and remarry was not a mere romantic reconciliation. It was a conscious choice, stemming from a deeper understanding and respect for each other's individuality. Their story beautifully encapsulates the essence of 'Married but Happily Single' – a philosophy that advocates for the coexistence of personal growth and marital commitment. It is a narrative that challenges the traditional notions of marriage, urging couples to view their union not as a merging of identities but as a partnership of distinct individuals.

Meera and Raj's journey is a powerful message to couples who find themselves struggling in their marital life. It emphasizes that marriage should not be a battleground for dominance or a sacrificial altar for personal dreams. Instead, it should be a nurturing ground for mutual growth, understanding, and respect.

As the author, I wish to convey through their story that the success of a marriage is not measured by the absence of conflict or the depth of sacrifice. It is determined by the ability of the partners to grow individually and together, to respect each other's space and dreams, and to find joy in each other's happiness. 'Married but Happily Single' is a call to embrace this balanced approach to marriage, where being together does not mean losing oneself, but rather, finding a new and shared path to fulfilment and success.

Closing Remarks by Author Arroon Gawalli: Embracing the Paradox of 'Married but Happily Single' - A Beacon of Hope

In the dynamic backdrop of Mumbai, a city that pulsates with countless stories of love, loss, and renewal, the journey of Meera and Raj unfolds—a saga that speaks to every heart that has experienced the pangs of marital discord or the deep scars of divorce. As your author, Arroon Gawalli, I wish to extend beyond their narrative, reaching out to you who are navigating these turbulent waters, offering a message of hope, resilience, and the transformative power of understanding and self-discovery.

'Married but Happily Single' is not just a story; it is a profound concept, a guiding philosophy for those embroiled in the complexities of marriage and divorce in our Indian society. It advocates for a harmonious balance between the shared path of marriage and the invaluable journey of individual self-realization.

To those in the throes of marital difficulties or on the precipice of divorce, I offer these heartfelt insights, drawn from the lives of Meera and Raj:

Embrace the Power of Open Communication: Always remember, dialogue is the thread that mends the fabric of a strained relationship. Honesty, empathy, and openness in communication are the cornerstones of understanding and reconciliation.

Hold Onto Your Individual Identity: Your uniqueness is your greatest asset. In the union of marriage, cherish and nurture your individuality. It is the strength of two strong, independent individuals that fortifies a relationship.

Seek Help, It's a Strength: There is immense courage in seeking help. Whether through counseling, therapy, or confiding in trusted friends, external support can offer new perspectives and healing.

Rise Above Societal Judgments: Society often casts a shadow over personal choices in marriage and divorce. Stand tall against these judgments; your journey is yours alone, to tread and to cherish.

Prioritize Personal Growth and Healing: Your emotional and spiritual growth is paramount. It is the foundation upon which a healthy life and, in turn, a healthy relationship is built.

Set Realistic Expectations: Disappointment often stems from unmet expectations. Embrace the reality of your partner's and your own capabilities and limitations. Understanding and acceptance pave the way to contentment.

Cultivate Forgiveness, It Heals: Forgiveness is a gift you give yourself and your partner. It is the balm that heals wounds and rekindles love and respect.

Be Thoughtful in Your Decisions: Whether considering marriage or contemplating divorce, give yourself the grace of time and reflection. Hasty decisions often lead to lasting regrets.

Be Open to Redefining Relationships: Life is fluid, and so are relationships. Be open to rekindling old sparks or reshaping your life post-divorce. New beginnings can be as beautiful as cherished memories.

Never Compromise on Self-Love and Respect: In the midst of emotional upheaval, never lose sight of your worth. You deserve love and respect, most importantly, from yourself.

As I conclude this narrative, I want to assure every reader, who might be struggling with the pain of a troubled marriage or the aftermath of a divorce, that there is a path to healing and happiness. Let the story of Meera and Raj be a testament to the fact that even in the darkest of times, there is a light of hope. Their journey exemplifies that it's possible to emerge from the shadows of pain and misunderstanding to a place of mutual respect, understanding, and love.

'Married but Happily Single' is a clarion call to find harmony in togetherness and in individuality. It's an encouragement to forge a relationship that respects personal space and cherishes joint growth. It's a narrative that reassures you that whether you choose to walk together or apart, you can still find fulfillment and joy.

In your journey of marriage or in the solitary path post-divorce, may you find the strength to face challenges with grace, the courage to make the right choices, and the wisdom to find peace in whatever path you choose. Remember, your story doesn't end with a difficult chapter; sometimes, it's just the beginning of a new narrative, one filled with hope, growth, and the promise of a happier tomorrow.

Thank you for joining me in this journey of discovery through the lives of Meera and Raj. May their story inspire you to write your own, marked by courage, love, and an enduring belief in the possibility of a life that's both individually fulfilling and harmoniously shared. May you find your own unique rhythm in the dance of 'Married but Happily Single'.

www.ingramcontent.com/pod-product-compliance
Lightning Source LLC
LaVergne TN
LVHW091538070526
838199LV00002B/107